PRAYERS
OF
REST

JOURNAL

60-DAY PRAYER JOURNAL

THIS JOURNAL BELONGS TO

_____

START DATE

_____

COMPLETED DATE

_____

Truly my soul finds rest in God.

– Psalm 62:1a, NIV

DO YOU GET DISTRACTED WHEN YOU PRAY?

You are not alone!

A recent survey from Crossway revealed that the number one obstacle to a thriving prayer life is distraction.[1]

You've experienced this too, haven't you? You start praying, but soon you're thinking about your grocery shopping, the laundry that needs switched into the dryer, the friend whose birthday is coming up… basically everything BUT your conversation with God.

And not only that, but it's also easy to feel like we don't quite know what to say. Our prayer time can easily become a wish list that we present to God like we're talking to a genie, and then we feel bad because we know that's not how we should approach prayer. But we don't how else to pray, and we feel too busy to figure it out, so pretty soon we stop praying altogether.

I get it. Even though I grew up in a Christian home and I'm now a Bible teacher and published author, I've struggled with my prayer life too. As a wife and mom to three young children (currently ages six and under), it's easy to put off prayer until "some day" when my life slows down. But I've found that I need the rest found only in God's presence—and I want to know and love Him more *now*, not wait until "some day" that may never come.

So I've resolved to seek God here and now—right in the middle of the chaos. I'm still on this journey just like you, and I want to share with you a prayer format that I've found helpful. That's why I created this journal.

Prayers of REST is a simple prayer format that guides you through praying God's Word using the following acronym:

R: Recite God's Goodness

E: Express Your Neediness

S: Seek His Stillness

T: Trust His Faithfulness

For years I prayed this way by myself, but in the spring of 2020, when the COVID-19 crisis hit the world and we all found ourselves isolated at home, I reached out to my Instagram followers and asked if they wanted to wake up early each morning to join me for Prayers of REST. They did.

So we prayed.

For eight weeks straight, every weekday morning, dozens of women from around the world gathered virtually to pray God's Word over our hearts and our homes. And God did something incredible—He brought peace, joy, and even rest into our lives during a global pandemic.

We learn how to pray not by reading a book or listening to a sermon (though those may prove helpful), but by actually praying. That's exactly what we did for those eight weeks, and that is what I hope this journal helps you do too.

You can use this journal on its own or as a companion to the *Prayers of REST* podcast. This journal, the podcast, and the Bible Study all came out of those live prayer calls, and they're a humble invitation to anyone who wants to experience God's rest in prayer. Find them all at www.prayersofrest.com.

Prayer is how we enter into God's rest. Throughout Scripture, God invites us to be still with Him, to know Him, and to find rest in Him (see Psalm 62:1,5). On the next pages, you'll find a list of Bible verses on the topic of rest; feel free to use these passages to prompt your Prayers of REST, or follow a reading plan of your choosing.

However you use this prayer journal, I hope you'll begin to experience the rest Jesus offered His disciples when He said: "Come with me by yourselves to a quiet place and get some rest." (Mark 6:31 NIV)

So we come to Him and rest in Him. And when our minds wander, we bring our attention back to Him, using the prompts on the page and the pen in our hands. I'm grateful we serve a compassionate God who welcomes us into His presence every day.

May I pray a blessing over you as we close?

Now to Him who is able to keep you from stumbling, and to present you before His glorious presence without fault and with great joy, to the only God our Savior be glory and majesty, power and authority through Jesus Christ our Lord, before all ages, now, and forevermore. Amen (Jude 24-25, NIV)

Asheritah

---

1) *How Is Your Prayer Life?" Crossway*, November 2, 2019.
   https://www.crossway.org/articles/infographic-how-is-your-prayer-life/.

RECITE
GOD'S GOODNESS

EXPRESS
YOUR NEEDINESS

SEEK
HIS STILLNESS

TRUST
HIS FAITHFULNESS

R E S T

40 SCRIPTURES ON REST

- ○ Matthew 11:28-29 *
- ○ Genesis 2:1-3
- ○ Exodus 20:8-11
- ○ Psalm 46:1-3 *
- ○ Psalm 46:10-11
- ○ Isaiah 26:3-4
- ○ Mark 6:30-31
- ○ Philippians 2:5-11 *
- ○ Isaiah 32:17-18
- ○ Psalm 4:7-8
- ○ Zephaniah 3:17 *
- ○ Exodus 33:12-14
- ○ Hebrews 4:14-16
- ○ Psalm 127:1-2
- ○ John 10:9-11 *
- ○ Proverbs 19:23
- ○ Psalm 4:3-4
- ○ Isaiah 37:16-17 *
- ○ John 14:27
- ○ Galatians 5:1

- ○ Psalm 62:1-8
- ○ Romans 8:26-27 *
- ○ Psalm 91:1-4
- ○ Mark 2:27-28
- ○ Mark 4:35-41 *
- ○ Psalm 3:3-5
- ○ Philippians 4:6-7
- ○ Proverbs 3:24
- ○ Isaiah 30:15-18 *
- ○ Romans 15:13
- ○ Psalm 73:25-28
- ○ John 15:9-13 *
- ○ John 16:33
- ○ Psalm 34:10
- ○ Matthew 8:23-27
- ○ Colossians 1:15-17 *
- ○ Psalm 23:1-4
- ○ 1 Chronicles 16:10-12
- ○ Isaiah 40:30-31
- ○ Revelation 21:3-7 *

*passages correspond to successive weeks of the Prayers of REST podcast
(available at www.prayersofrest.com).*

[Jot down a verse or two from today's Scripture reading that you want to focus your prayer on today.]

Recite
God's Goodness

[Begin by reciting God's goodness, praising Him for who He is and what He has done. Remind yourself what is true about His character. What do you see in the Scriptures that you want to praise Him for?]

Express
Your Neediness

[Take time to express your neediness. Confess to God how you have failed to love Him and/or to love your neighbor. Receive His forgiveness, and ask Him to help you live as He desires.]

Prayer is putting oneself in the hands of God, at His disposition,
and listening to His voice in the depth of our hearts.

———

MOTHER TERESA

Seek
His Stillness

[Take a few minutes to become aware of God's loving presence surrounding you this very moment. Allow His peace to fill you, His love to surround you. Just be with your Heavenly Father. Write down anything you feel He is saying to you.]

Trust
His Faithfulness

[Finally, trust God's faithfulness. Preach the gospel to yourself, and then declare your confidence in God that He will take care of the burdens you entrust to Him. End by declaring out loud: "God I trust You. I trust that You will be faithful."]

Because of his great love for us, God, who is rich in mercy, made us alive with Christ even when we were dead in transgressions-it is by grace you have been saved. And God raised us up with Christ and seated us with him in the heavenly realms in Christ Jesus, in order that in the coming ages he might show the incomparable riches of his grace, expressed in his kindness to us in Christ Jesus

R Recite
God's Goodness

God, You are rich in mercy and You've shown such great love toward me! It wasn't my beauty or perfection that attracted You to me, because You saved me while I was still dead in my sin-not because I deserved it, but to display Your immeasurable riches in your kindness toward me in Christ Jesus. What a kind and compassionate God You are!

E Express
Your Neediness

Lord God, You call me to live into my present heavenly reality of being made alive in Christ, but I need Your help. Through the power of the Spirit who raised Jesus from the dead, help me to put to death my old nature. Help me stop lashing out in anger to my children, or drowning my sorrows in a pint of ice cream, or escaping my daily tedium by scrolling my phone. All those things used to characterize me, but I want to live the victorious and conquering life You promise as I walk in step with the Spirit. Help me, God.

S Seek
His Stillness

. . .

Thank You, God, that I am chosen, not forsaken. I am who You say I am. Help me to remember that and live that way.

. . .

T Trust
His Faithfulness

God, You are steadfast in Your faithful love, not giving up on the humans You created but bringing redemption at great cost to Your very life. It is You I adore. You are faithful, and You will complete the good work that You started in me. Help me to live today not with the burden of self-improvement, but resting in the reality of Your sanctifying work in my life.
I am free to say "yes" to the Spirit and "no" to my flesh, not by my own power but by Your Spirit's power at work in me. I trust You, God.

Amen.

Bible Passage: /   /

R Recite
God's Goodness

E Express
Your Neediness

The more we pray, the more we think to pray, and as we see the results of prayer—the responses of our Father to our requests—our confidence in God's power spills over into other areas of our life.

———

DALLAS WILLARD

Seek
His Stillness

Trust
His Faithfulness

Bible Passage: /   /

R Recite
God's Goodness

E Express
Your Neediness

S Seek
His Stillness

T Trust
His Faithfulness

Bible Passage: /   /

R Recite
God's Goodness

E Express
Your Neediness

Prayer is the core of the day.
Take prayer out, and the day would collapse.

———

AMY CARMICHAEL

Seek
His Stillness

Trust
His Faithfulness

Bible Passage: /   /

R Recite
God's Goodness

E Express
Your Neediness

S Seek
His Stillness

T Trust
His Faithfulness

Bible Passage: /   /

R Recite
God's Goodness

E Express
Your Neediness

There is not in the world a kind of life more sweet and delightful, than that of a continual conversation with God; those only can comprehend it who practice and experience it.

———

BROTHER LAWRENCE

Seek
His Stillness

Trust
His Faithfulness

Bible Passage: /   /

R Recite
God's Goodness

E Express
Your Neediness

S **Seek**
His Stillness

T **Trust**
His Faithfulness

Bible Passage: /   /

R Recite
God's Goodness

E Express
Your Neediness

One can believe intellectually in the efficacy of prayer and never do any praying.

———

CATHERINE MARSHALL

Seek
His Stillness

Trust
His Faithfulness

Bible Passage: / /

Recite
God's Goodness

Express
Your Neediness

S Seek
His Stillness

T Trust
His Faithfulness

Bible Passage: /   /

R Recite
God's Goodness

E Express
Your Neediness

Always respond to every impulse to pray. The impulse to pray may come when you are reading or when you are battling with a text.
I would make an absolute law of this: always obey such an impulse.

———

MARTYN LLOYD-JONES

Seek
His Stillness

Trust
His Faithfulness

Bibles Passage: /   /

R Recite
God's Goodness

E Express
Your Neediness

Seek
His Stillness

Trust
His Faithfulness

Bible Passage: /   /

R Recite
God's Goodness

E Express
Your Neediness

Prayer keeps us in constant communion with God, which is the goal of our entire believing lives. Without a doubt, prayerless lives are powerless lives, and prayerful lives are powerful lives; but, believe it or not, the ultimate goal God has for us is not power but personal intimacy with Him.

───

BETH MOORE

Seek
His Stillness

Trust
His Faithfulness

Bible Passage: /   /

R Recite
God's Goodness

E Express
Your Neediness

S **Seek**
His Stillness

T **Trust**
His Faithfulness

Bible Passage: /   /

R Recite
God's Goodness

E Express
Your Neediness

The lover of silence draws close to God.
He talks to Him in secret and God enlightens him.

———

JOHN CLIMACUS

Seek
His Stillness

Trust
His Faithfulness

Bible Passage: /   /

R Recite
God's Goodness

E Express
Your Neediness

Seek
His Stillness

Trust
His Faithfulness

Bible Passage: /   /

R Recite
God's Goodness

E Express
Your Neediness

Prayer will illuminate the difference between
knowing God's will and guessing about it.

———

BECKY TIRABASSI

S **Seek**
His Stillness

T **Trust**
His Faithfulness

Bible Passage: /   /

R Recite
God's Goodness

E Express
Your Neediness

S **Seek**
His Stillness

T **Trust**
His Faithfulness

Bible Passage: /   /

R **Recite**
God's Goodness

E **Express**
Your Neediness

Give over your restlessness and effort; fall helpless at the feet of the Lord Jesus;
He will speak the word, and your soul will live. If we recognize that a right relationship to
the Lord Jesus, above all else, includes prayer, then we have something
which gives us the right to rejoice in Him and rest in Him.

———

ANDREW MURRAY

S Seek
His Stillness

T Trust
His Faithfulness

Bible Passage: /   /

R Recite
God's Goodness

E Express
Your Neediness

S **Seek**
His Stillness

T **Trust**
His Faithfulness

Bible Passage: /   /

R Recite
God's Goodness

E Express
Your Neediness

It's almost impossible to hear the voice of God when you're constantly hearing your own chatter. When I come to my secret place to meet with God, I try to block out everything that will distract me. I fall to my knees and ask God to teach me to be still.

LINDA DILLOW

Seek
His Stillness

Trust
His Faithfulness

R Recite
God's Goodness

E Express
Your Neediness

S Seek
His Stillness

T Trust
His Faithfulness

Bible Passage: /   /

R Recite
God's Goodness

E Express
Your Neediness

Prayer is not so much an act as it is an attitude;
an attitude of dependency, dependency upon God.

———

ARTHUR W. PINK

Seek
His Stillness

Trust
His Faithfulness

Bible Passage: /   /

R Recite
God's Goodness

E Express
Your Neediness

S **Seek**
His Stillness

T **Trust**
His Faithfulness

Bible Passage: /   /

R Recite
God's Goodness

E Express
Your Neediness

Prayer isn't about getting what you desperately want,
but about getting more of the One who desperately wants you.

———

ANN VOSKAMP

Seek
His Stillness

Trust
His Faithfulness

Bible Passage: /   /

R Recite
God's Goodness

E Express
Your Neediness

S Seek
His Stillness

T Trust
His Faithfulness

Bible Passage: /   /

R Recite
God's Goodness

E Express
Your Neediness

Ten minutes spent in the presence of Christ every day, aye, two minutes,
will make the whole day different.

———

HENRY DRUMMOND

Seek
His Stillness

Trust
His Faithfulness

Bible Passage: /   /

R Recite
God's Goodness

E Express
Your Neediness

S Seek
His Stillness

T Trust
His Faithfulness

Bible Passage: /   /

R Recite
God's Goodness

E Express
Your Neediness

There is no promise too hard for God to fulfill.
No prayer is too big for Him to answer.

———

CHRISTINE CAINE

Seek
His Stillness

Trust
His Faithfulness

Bible Passage: /   /

R Recite
God's Goodness

E Express
Your Neediness

S **Seek**
His Stillness

T **Trust**
His Faithfulness

Bible Passage: /   /

R Recite
God's Goodness

E Express
Your Neediness

Prayer requires some discipline, yet I believe that life with God should seem more like friendship than duty. Prayer includes moments of ecstasy and also dullness, mindless distraction and acute concentration, flashes of joy and bouts of irritation.
In other words, prayer has features in common with all relationships that matter.

———

PHILIP YANCEY

Seek
His Stillness

Trust
His Faithfulness

Bible Passage: /   /

R Recite
God's Goodness

E Express
Your Neediness

S Seek
His Stillness

T Trust
His Faithfulness

Bible Passage: /   /

R Recite
God's Goodness

E Express
Your Neediness

*I will tell you what rule I observed when I was young,
and too much addicted to childish diversions: never to spend more time in mere
recreation in one day than I spent in private religious devotions.*

―――

SUSANNA WESLEY

Seek
His Stillness

Trust
His Faithfulness

Bibles Passage: /   /

R Recite
God's Goodness

E Express
Your Neediness

S Seek
His Stillness

T Trust
His Faithfulness

Bibical Passage: /   /

R Recite
God's Goodness

E Express
Your Neediness

The engagement of the heart in worship is the coming alive of the feelings and emotions and affections of the heart. Where feelings for God are dead, worship is dead.

———

JOHN PIPER

 **Seek**
His Stillness

 **Trust**
His Faithfulness

Bible Passage: /   /

R **Recite**
God's Goodness

E **Express**
Your Neediness

S **Seek**
His Stillness

T **Trust**
His Faithfulness

Bible Passage: /   /

R Recite
God's Goodness

E Express
Your Neediness

Prayer is not about the right words;
it's about the right heart.

———

SHEILA WALSH

Seek
His Stillness

Trust
His Faithfulness

Bible Passage: /   /

R Recite
God's Goodness

E Express
Your Neediness

S Seek
His Stillness

T Trust
His Faithfulness

Bibliography Passage: /   /

R **Recite**
God's Goodness

E **Express**
Your Neediness

To have God speak to the heart is a majestic experience, an experience that people may miss if they monopolize the conversation and never pause to hear God's responses.

——

CHARLES STANLEY

Seek
His Stillness

Trust
His Faithfulness

Bible Passage: /   /

R Recite
God's Goodness

E Express
Your Neediness

S Seek
His Stillness

T Trust
His Faithfulness

Bible Passage: /   /

R **Recite**
God's Goodness

E **Express**
Your Neediness

Prayer is not eloquence, but earnestness; not the definition of helplessness,
but the feeling of it; not figures of speech, but earnestness of soul.

———

HANNAH MORE

Seek
His Stillness

Trust
His Faithfulness

Bible Passage: /   /

R Recite
God's Goodness

E Express
Your Neediness

S Seek
His Stillness

T Trust
His Faithfulness

Bible Passage: /   /

R Recite
God's Goodness

E Express
Your Neediness

Pray when you feel like praying. Pray when you don't feel like praying.
Pray until you feel like praying
———

ELISABETH ELLIOT

 **Seek**
His Stillness

 **Trust**
His Faithfulness

Bible Passage: /   /

R Recite
God's Goodness

E Express
Your Neediness

S Seek
His Stillness

T Trust
His Faithfulness

Bible Passage: /   /

R Recite
God's Goodness

E Express
Your Neediness

To pray, I think, does not mean to think about God in contrast to thinking about other things, or to spend time with God instead of spending time with other people. Rather, it means to think and live in the presence of God.

——

HENRI NOUWEN

Seek
His Stillness

Trust
His Faithfulness

Bible Passage: /   /

R **Recite**
God's Goodness

E **Express**
Your Neediness

S Seek
His Stillness

T Trust
His Faithfulness

Bible Passage: /   /

R Recite
God's Goodness

E Express
Your Neediness

This way of prayer, this simple relationship to your Lord, is so suited for everyone; it is just as suited for the dull and the ignorant as it is for the well-educated. This prayer, this experience which begins so simply, has as its end a totally abandoned love to the Lord. Only one thing is required—Love.

————

MADAME GUYON

Seek
His Stillness

Trust
His Faithfulness

Bible Passage: /   /

R Recite
God's Goodness

E Express
Your Neediness

S **Seek**
His Stillness

T **Trust**
His Faithfulness

Bible Passage: /   /

R **Recite**
God's Goodness

E **Express**
Your Neediness

Any concern too small to be turned into a prayer
is too small to be made into a burden.

———

CORRIE TEN BOOM

Seek
His Stillness

Trust
His Faithfulness

Bible Passage: /   /

R Recite
God's Goodness

E Express
Your Neediness

S **Seek**
His Stillness

T **Trust**
His Faithfulness

Bible Passage: /   /

R Recite
God's Goodness

E Express
Your Neediness

You may pray for an hour and still not pray.
You may meet God for a moment and then be in touch with Him all day.

———

FREDRIK WISLOFF

Seek
His Stillness

Trust
His Faithfulness

Bible Passage: /   /

R Recite
God's Goodness

E Express
Your Neediness

S Seek
His Stillness

T Trust
His Faithfulness

Bible Passage: /   /

R   **Recite**
    God's Goodness

E   **Express**
    Your Neediness

Be a prayer warrior—not a panicked worrier.

———

ANN VOSKAMP

S Seek
His Stillness

T Trust
His Faithfulness

Bible Passage: /   /

R Recite
God's Goodness

E Express
Your Neediness

S **Seek**
His Stillness

T **Trust**
His Faithfulness

Bible Passage: /   /

R Recite
God's Goodness

E Express
Your Neediness

*Prayer is simply asking God to do for us what he has promised us he will do
if we ask him. Asking is man's part. Giving is God's part. The praying belongs to us.
The answer belongs to God.*

———

GERHARD TERSTEEGEN

Seek
His Stillness

Trust
His Faithfulness

Bible Passage: /   /

R Recite
God's Goodness

E Express
Your Neediness

S **Seek**
His Stillness

T **Trust**
His Faithfulness

Bible Passage: /   /

R Recite
God's Goodness

E Express
Your Neediness

You write out your prayers so you "won't forget": won't forget who the real enemy is, won't forget the One in whom your hope lies, won't forget what your real need and dependencies are, and later, won't forget the record of how God responds.

———

PRISCILLA SHIRER

S Seek
His Stillness

T Trust
His Faithfulness

Bible Passage: /   /

R Recite
God's Goodness

E Express
Your Neediness

S **Seek**
His Stillness

T **Trust**
His Faithfulness

Bible Passage: /   /

R Recite
God's Goodness

E Express
Your Neediness

We do not need more of the Holy Spirit.
He needs more of us.

———

MARK BUBEK

S **Seek**
His Stillness

T **Trust**
His Faithfulness

Bibliography Passage: /   /

R **Recite**
  God's Goodness

E **Express**
  Your Neediness

S Seek
His Stillness

T Trust
His Faithfulness

Bible Passage: / /

R Recite
God's Goodness

E Express
Your Neediness

Sometimes the most powerful prayers are the most simple prayers.

———

LYSA TERKEURST

S Seek
His Stillness

T Trust
His Faithfulness

Bible Passage: /   /

R Recite
God's Goodness

E Express
Your Neediness

S **Seek**
His Stillness

T **Trust**
His Faithfulness

ABOUT THE AUTHOR

Asheritah Ciuciu is a bestselling writer and speaker, wife to her high school sweetheart Flaviu and mama to three spunky kiddos. She grew up in Romania as a missionary kid and studied English and Women's Ministry at Cedarville University. Her passion is helping overwhelmed women find joy in Jesus through creative and consistent time in God's Word. Download your free guide to *Cultivate Consistent Quiet Time with Jesus* at www.OneThingAlone.com.

MORE
BOOKS FROM ASHERITAH

Scan this QR code
or go to **asheritah.com/books**
to find more books from Asheritah.

DO YOU GET DISTRACTED WHEN YOU PRAY?

Learn how to focus your heart and mind in prayer and experience the refreshing rest only God can offer in this new 6-week Bible study from Asheritah. It's perfect to study on your own or with a small group; order today on Amazon or www.asheritah.com/books.

*Full: Food, Jesus, and the Battle
for Satisfaction*

*Bible & Breakfast:
31 Mornings with Jesus*

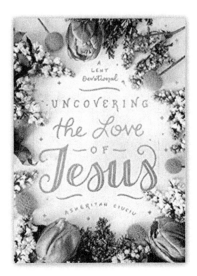

*Uncovering the Love of Jesus:
A Lent Devotional*

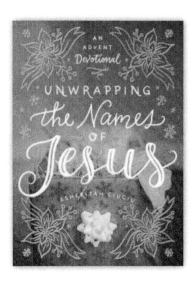

*Unwrapping the Names of Jesus:
An Advent Devotional*

Quiet Time Journal:
90-Day Bible Study and Prayer Journal

He is Enough:
Living in the Fullness of Jesus

Quiet Time for Busy Women:
6 Weeks to Becoming Consistent
in Your Daily Devotions

Walking with God:
Enjoying God's Presence from
Morning to Night

Printed in Great Britain
by Amazon